SPACE TECHNOLOGY

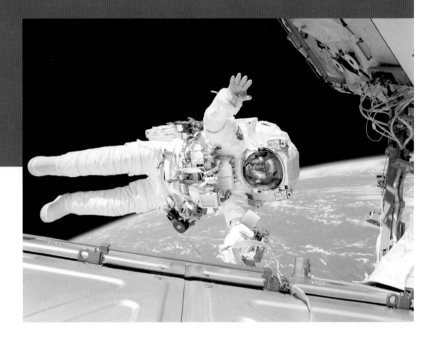

Linda Bruce,
John Hilvert, and
Jack Bruce

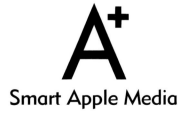

Smart Apple Media

Smart Apple Media
2140 Howard Drive West
North Mankato
Minnesota 56003

First published in 2005 by
MACMILLAN EDUCATION AUSTRALIA PTY LTD
627 Chapel Street, South Yarra, Australia 3141

Visit our Web site at www.macmillan.com.au

Associated companies and representatives throughout the world.

Library of Congress Cataloging-in-Publication Data

Bruce, Linda.
   Space technology / by Linda Bruce.
      p. cm. – (How does it work?)
   Includes index.
   ISBN-13: 978-1-58340-795-0 (hc : alk. Paper)
   1. Space vehicles—Juvenile literature. 2. Aerospace engineering—Juvenile literature. I. Title. II. Series.

TI.793.B765 2006
629.1--dc22

                                                                                          2005046787

Edited by Anna Fern
Text and cover design by Modern Art Production Group
Illustrations by Andrew Louey
Photo research by Legend Images

Printed in USA

Acknowledgments
The author and publishers are grateful to the following for permission to reproduce copyright material:

Cover photo: Astronaut, courtesy of NASA/Human Space Flight.

Digital Vision, page 27; NASA, pages 5, 28; NASA/Human Space Flight, pages 1, 8, 9, 10, 14, 18, 30; NASA/JPL/Cornell, page 23; NASA/JSC, page 22; Photodisc, page 26; Photolibrary.com/SPL, pages 7, 11, 12, 13, 15, 19, 20, 21, 24, 25, 29; Photos.com, page 4; Picture Media/Reuters/Mike Blake, page 16; Picture Media/Reuters/Jim Campbell/Areo News Network/POO, page 17.

While every care has been taken to trace and acknowledge copyright, the publisher tenders their apologies for any accidental infringement where copyright has proved untraceable. Where the attempt has been unsuccessful, the publisher welcomes information that would redress the situation.

Contents

Glossary words

When a word is printed in **bold**, you can look up its meaning in the Glossary on page 31.

What is technology?

Technology helps us to do things. Technology is also about how things work. Since ancient times, people have been interested in how things work, and how they can improve technology to meet their needs. They use their experience, knowledge, and ideas to invent new ways of doing things.

The *How Does It Work?* series features the design and technology of machines that are part of our daily lives. This includes:

- the purpose of the technology and its design
- where it is used
- how it is used
- materials it is made from
- how it works
- future developments

Technology has changed the way we live in many ways. It will keep on bringing change, as people constantly invent new ways of doing things using new materials.

Space technology, such as telescopes, enables people to explore space.

4

Space technology

A blanket of air about 62 to 74 miles (100 to 120 km) thick surrounds Earth. Beyond that is space. Even though space is so close, it is difficult to travel there because, to escape the pull of Earth's **gravity** and reach **Earth orbit**, machines must travel at 17,000 miles (28,000 km) per hour. To venture farther and escape the pull of Earth's gravity completely, machines must go even faster, reaching an **escape velocity** of 25,000 miles (40,000 km) per hour. This takes a huge amount of energy.

During the last 100 years, new technology has revolutionized space exploration. Rockets and fuels have been invented to carry machines into space. Capsules, shuttles, space planes, and space stations provide places for astronauts to live and work. Landers and rovers, many of them remote controlled, have enabled exploration of the surfaces of Earth's **moon** and Mars, and probes and telescopes collect information on the far reaches of space.

This book takes an inside look at different kinds of space technology. It also previews some amazing new developments in space technology that will help us to learn more about the universe.

This photograph was taken on Mars by a remote-controlled space rover.

Rockets

A rocket is a machine propelled by gas escaping from nozzles at the bottom.

Where used?

Large rockets are used to transport space capsules, shuttles, satellites, probes, and other machines into space. Smaller rockets are used to move machines once they are in space.

How used?

Rockets are containers full of liquid or solid fuel. Liquid fuel rockets are easier to control, because they can be switched on and off. They are the main rockets used to launch space capsules and shuttles. Solid-fuel rockets are used to help boost rockets into space. Once lit, they cannot be turned off.

Materials

Rockets are mostly made of strong, lightweight metal **alloys**. Rocket fuels include hydrogen, nitrogen, kerosene, and alcohol, which are mixed with liquid oxygen.

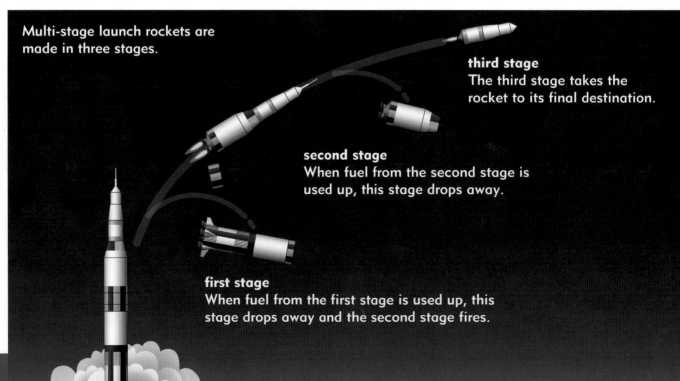

Multi-stage launch rockets are made in three stages.

third stage
The third stage takes the rocket to its final destination.

second stage
When fuel from the second stage is used up, this stage drops away.

first stage
When fuel from the first stage is used up, this stage drops away and the second stage fires.

How rockets work

To travel at 17,000 miles (28,000 km) per hour to blast into space, rockets carry an enormous amount of fuel. As the rocket rises, the air thins and there is not enough oxygen for fuel to mix with to be able to burn. Therefore, rockets also carry liquid oxygen. Rockets travel from launch pad to space in 9 to 12 minutes.

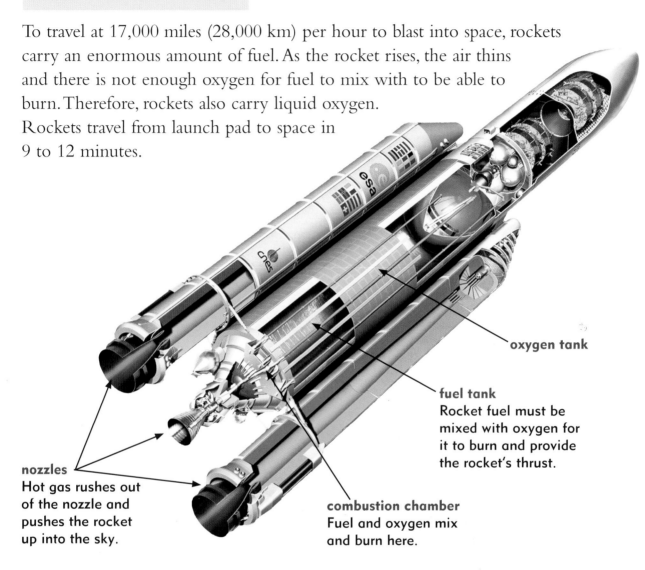

oxygen tank

fuel tank
Rocket fuel must be mixed with oxygen for it to burn and provide the rocket's thrust.

nozzles
Hot gas rushes out of the nozzle and pushes the rocket up into the sky.

combustion chamber
Fuel and oxygen mix and burn here.

What's next?

In the future, rockets may speed faster and farther. They will be fueled by solar power, or a mixture of hydrogen and helium collected on their journey through space. Rockets will also become safer. **NASA** engineers have designed an air-breathing rocket that burns fuel with oxygen from Earth's **atmosphere** when it first blasts off. When oxygen becomes scarce, the rocket switches to burning fuel with oxygen carried by the rocket. This will minimize the risk of the rocket exploding, and reduce launch costs.

Capsules

Space capsules are used to carry animals and people into space and back. Space capsules are the most commonly used passenger spacecraft. They are about the size of a small car.

Where used?

Capsules are launched from Earth, travel to space and other **planets**, and then parachute back to Earth, landing either in the sea or on land.

How used?

The capsule is attached to a rocket to be launched into space from Earth. A Soyuz capsule, one of the most modern and safe capsules available, is permanently docked at the International Space Station, ready to evacuate crews in the event of an emergency. Capsules cost less to fly and are safer than space shuttles, but are not able to carry as much as shuttles. However, because several space-shuttle missions have ended in disaster, capsules have become the main space passenger vehicle.

Materials

Capsules are made from lightweight metal alloys. **Insulating** material in the walls and on the heat shield prevents overheating on re-entry to Earth's atmosphere.

On October 31 2000, the first permanent crew of the International Space Station rode to the space station in a Russian Soyuz capsule.

How do capsules work?

Once the capsule reaches orbital height, the last stage of the rocket launcher falls off. The capsule then adjusts its height and speed by firing small rocket thrusters. When the capsule re-enters Earth's atmosphere, a parachute helps it slow down before landing.

Capsules re-enter Earth's atmosphere at approximately 11,000 miles (17,000 km) per hour, curved end first. Friction from the atmosphere makes it very hot. To protect the crew, capsules are insulated with special materials. Capsules also have a shield of heat-resistant plastic, which burns away.

This Soyuz capsule is departing from the International Space Station to return to Earth.

What's next?

Soyuz capsules last only one mission, so NASA is building a reusable capsule to ferry astronauts to and from the International Space Station.

Shuttles

Space shuttles are reusable planes that transport people and machines into space. Also called orbiters, space shuttles have been transporting astronauts into space since 1977.

Where used?

A space shuttle blasts off from Earth, orbits Earth, and then glides back to Earth. It carries passengers and cargo, such as satellites and space station parts, to space. In space, it opens its cargo bay to place satellites in orbit or pull them on board for repairs.

How used?

A space shuttle carries a typical crew of seven. It has a large **payload** bay to carry supplies to the space station and machines, such as satellites. Space shuttles orbit Earth at approximately 17,000 miles (28,000 km) per hour. They circle Earth in 1.5 hours. Space shuttle missions last 7 to 14 days.

Materials

Shuttles are mainly made from light, strong metal alloys. Insulating ceramic tiles are used on the outside to help stop the metal from melting, and the astronauts from overheating.

fuel tank

orbiter
The orbiter carries the astronauts and payload.

rocket
Two solid rocket boosters, one on each side of an external fuel tank, launch the shuttle.

The space shuttle *Atlantis* was launched in 2002.

How do space shuttles work?

The shuttle launches by firing its three built-in engines, and two solid rocket boosters. Combined, these engines produce as much power as 30 jumbo jets. The rockets burn for two minutes, boosting the shuttle 28 miles (45 km) high, at 3,088 miles (4,973 km) per hour. Empty rockets drop back into the ocean. The shuttle reaches space in nine minutes. It throws off its external fuel tank, which falls back toward Earth and burns up on re-entry into the atmosphere. The shuttle then accelerates to orbital speed. To re-enter, the pilot slows the shuttle and lowers its belly toward Earth. Then it glides back to base, landing at around 220 miles (350 km) per hour.

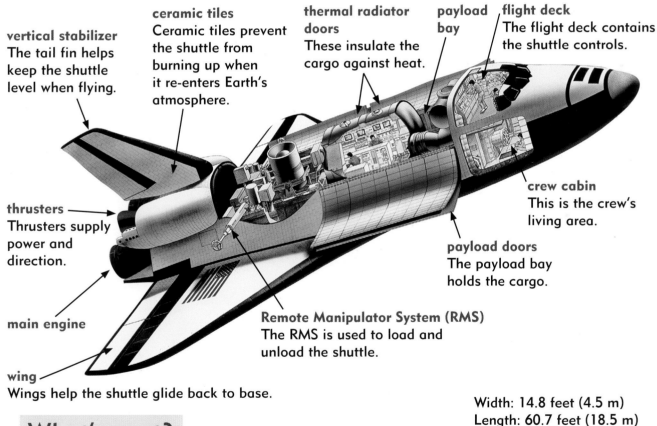

vertical stabilizer
The tail fin helps keep the shuttle level when flying.

ceramic tiles
Ceramic tiles prevent the shuttle from burning up when it re-enters Earth's atmosphere.

thermal radiator doors
These insulate the cargo against heat.

payload bay

flight deck
The flight deck contains the shuttle controls.

thrusters
Thrusters supply power and direction.

main engine

wing
Wings help the shuttle glide back to base.

Remote Manipulator System (RMS)
The RMS is used to load and unload the shuttle.

crew cabin
This is the crew's living area.

payload doors
The payload bay holds the cargo.

Width: 14.8 feet (4.5 m)
Length: 60.7 feet (18.5 m)

What's next?

In the future, unmanned robot shuttles will transport machines to space. Space lifts anchored on Earth and fixed to a satellite may transport people to space stations. Long, sloping space ramps may one day enable vehicles to drive to and from space.

Remote Manipulator Systems

A Remote Manipulator System (RMS) is used to do jobs, such as lifting machines out of space shuttles, and pulling satellites on board space shuttles for repairs.

Where used?

Also called robot arms, Remote Manipulator Systems are used on space shuttles and on the International Space Station *Freedom*, which has been under construction since 1996. Modules for the space station, which are like small rooms, are assembled on Earth and transported by shuttle to the space station.

How used?

Astronauts operate the RMS from inside the shuttle. Outside, workers tie their feet to the RMS and stand on it when they bolt space-station parts together. Video cameras on the RMS enable the operator to see what the RMS is doing.

Materials

The RMS is made from strong, lightweight metal alloys. Because these materials are light, it costs less to transport them. The heavier the item is, the more fuel and money it costs to take it into space.

Astronaut Woody Spring stands on the RMS while assembling the International Space Station.

How do Remote Manipulator Systems work?

The RMS arm can move and bend like a human arm, and can stretch out to 55 feet (17 m). The "hand" grabs or moves the payload. The two lightweight poles are called the upper and lower arms. The arm has four video camera eyes on it, two on the boom and the others on the "hand."

mobile base
The mobile base lets the RMS slide along the payload bay of a space shuttle, or along the outside of a space station.

shoulder joint

upper arm

elbow joint

lower arm

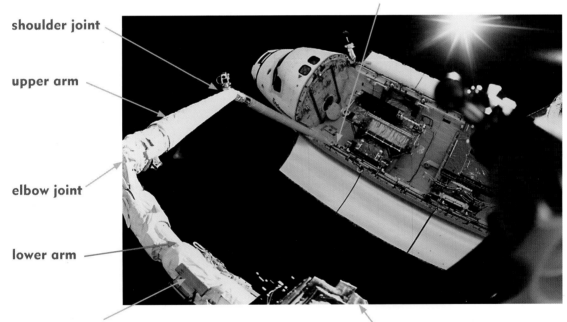

video cameras
Four cameras allow the people controlling the arm to see what they are doing.

hand unit
The hand unit is also called a "special purpose dextrous manipulator" (SPDM).

What's next?

In the future, robot arms will have built-in intelligence so that they will be able to recognize the parts of machines they are maneuvering. Space workers may drive around in space bubbles with mechanical arms with which they can perform work.

Space suits

A space suit, or extravehicular mobility unit (EMU), needs to be worn by an astronaut whenever they are outside their space shuttle, capsule, or station. A space suit creates an Earth-like environment, which protects the astronaut and keeps them alive.

Where used?

Space suits are used in space, where there is no oxygen and no air pressure. Without a space suit, humans would die within 15 seconds of leaving a spacecraft.

How used?

Space suits are made in sections that can be mixed and matched to fit individual astronauts. The astronauts put on the suits before leaving the spacecraft.

Materials

Space suits are made from special materials, such as nylon, dacron, gore-tex, and kevlar (the material in bullet-proof vests). These materials keep the body comfortable, and at the right temperature while the astronaut works.

Space suits keep astronauts safe and comfortable while they work.

How do space suits work?

A space suit contains equipment to keep the astronaut alive, and to enable the astronaut to communicate.

gloves
The suit has outer and inner gloves.

backpack and life support system
This includes oxygen, power, carbon dioxide removal, cooling water, radio equipment and the warning system.

maximum absorption garment
Two layers of material collect the astronaut's urine.

liquid cooling and ventilation garment
Two layers of material keep the astronaut cool.

helmet
Microphones and earphones enable the astronaut to communicate from inside the suit. The visor protects the astronaut's eyes from glare.

hard upper torso
This includes arms, torso, helmet, life-support backpack, and suit controls.

lower torso assembly
This includes pants, knee and ankle joints, boots, and lower waist.

What's next?

For missions to Mars, NASA is developing "hard suits" which are more flexible, durable, lightweight, and easier to put on than current space suits.

Space planes

A space plane can fly like a jet in Earth's atmosphere, and like a rocket in space. Three main types of space planes are currently being developed. The first is remote-controlled and carries no crew. The second is piggybacked 25 miles (40 km) high by a larger plane, called a space-bus or mother ship, then uses rocket engines to launch. The third, instead of using launch rockets, carries all fuel inside itself.

Where used?

Spaces planes will be used in Earth's atmosphere, as well as in space. They are cheaper, lighter, and safer than space shuttles.

How used?

Space planes will ferry passengers and supplies between Earth and space, or, flying at 8,000 miles (13,000 km) per hour, they may transport passengers from Sydney to London in 90 minutes. Other robot space planes will carry out explorations that may be dangerous for humans.

Materials

Space planes are made from lightweight strong metal alloys. To reduce heat that may melt them on re-entry into Earth's atmosphere, they are lined with heat-resistant ceramic tiles and plastics.

mother ship
The mother ship carries the space plane 25 miles (40 km) high.

fuel tank

rocket engine
At 25 miles (40 km) above Earth, the space plane fires its rocket engine to blast into space.

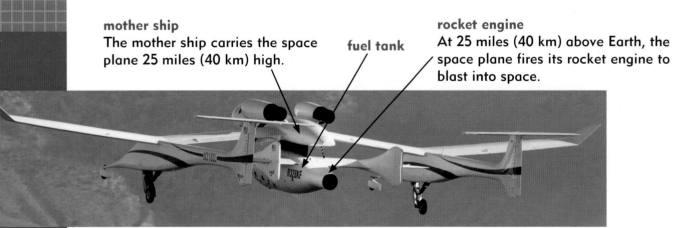

On June 21 2004, *SpaceShipOne* became the first privately owned space plane to fly to space.

How do space planes work?

There are three main types of space plane:

- The first type of space plane, such as SpaceShipOne or the sub-orbital X-34, has speeds of around 5,600 miles (9,000 km) per hour, which is not fast enough to orbit Earth. This plane is piggybacked on a larger jet to an altitude of 25 miles (40 km). It then uses rocket engines to blast into space
- The second type, such as the Russian Buran, operates without crew. It is carried to space on a rocket or shuttle, and its flight is controlled by radio signals sent from Earth
- The third type of space plane has a wedge-shaped design that allows the craft to hold all its fuel, eliminating the need for rocket boosters and an external tank. This cuts costs by reducing launch weight

rudders
The pilot moves the rudders to steer the plane.

wings
Wings enable the plane to glide back to base.

crew compartment
The crew compartment contains passenger seats and controls for the pilot.

main nozzle
Gas exits the nozzle to move the space plane.

rocket engine

fuel tank
Nitrous oxide fuels the rocket engine.

What's next?

In the future, space planes will take off from Earth using jet engines. When they reach a height where there is no longer enough oxygen to mix with the fuel, they will swap to rocket engines.

Space stations

Space stations provide a base for people to live and work in space. They are designed to stay in space for long periods. Since the 1970s, there have been eight space stations. The International Space Station Freedom is the only station currently in orbit.

Where used?

The International Space Station (ISS) orbits between 220 and 240 miles (350 and 390 km) above Earth, traveling at 4.8 miles (7.7 km) per second. Sixteen countries are cooperating to build the ISS—the United States, Canada, Japan, Brazil, and the European Space Agency countries of the United Kingdom, France, Germany, Belgium, Italy, Netherlands, Denmark, Norway, Spain, Switzerland, Sweden, and Russia.

How used?

Astronauts stay on space stations to perform experiments, learn about the effects of living in space, and test technology to improve living conditions in space.

Materials

The ISS is made from metal alloys which are light enough to transport to space, and strong enough to resist heat, cold, and bombardment by small particles. Reflective **aluminum** shields reduce the heat from the sun.

The ISS is 289 feet (88 m) long, 358 feet (109 m) wide, and 144 feet (44 m) high.

How the International Space Station works

In 1998, the first parts of the ISS were placed in orbit 250 miles (400 km) above Earth. Construction started with the launch of Russian and US modules. The completed station will have a 355-foot- (108-m-) long hexagon-shaped beam of metal alloys, called a truss. Room-like modules the size of a small school bus are bolted to the truss.

service module
The service module contains living quarters and life support equipment. When completed, the ISS will house seven astronauts.

Remote Manipulator System (RMS)
A robot arm will move along the outside of the station to conduct maintenance.

truss

scientific laboratories (six)

control module
Two rocket engine boosters help keep the ISS in orbit.

docking port
Transfer vehicles and emergency escape capsules dock here.

solar panels
Electrical power is generated by solar panels.

What's next?

In the future, stations may be stepping-stones for people traveling to other planets and moons. **Artificial** gravity will reduce space sickness, and tourists may visit space stations.

Space probes

A space probe is a remote-controlled machine which is used to explore the **solar system**. Space-probe missions can last many years.

Where used?

Space probes are transported from Earth to space by rocket or in a space shuttle. Once in orbit, space probes use their computer and rocket engines to travel to their destination, which may be on the outer edges of our **galaxy**, billions of miles away. With the exception of Pluto and the 10th planet **Quaoar**, probes have orbited all of the planets in our solar system.

How used?

Space probes record information and transmit this information back to Earth by radio and **laser**. Probes fly within a few thousand miles of their destination, and may orbit the planet or moon. While in orbit, a probe may send another vehicle, called a lander, to explore the surface of the planet or moon.

Materials

Probes are made from lightweight metal alloys, such as aluminum. Solar panels made from **silicon** are used to generate electricity.

The *Cassini* space probe, launched in 1997, reached Saturn on July 1 2004. This picture shows *Cassini* visiting Saturn's moon, Titan. A lander investigated Titan's surface.

How do space probes work?

Space probes are remote controlled from Earth. Their sensors and cameras send information back to **radio receivers** on Earth. The *Cassini* space probe has two main parts, the *Cassini* orbiter and the *Huygens* lander.

Rocket thrusters on *Cassini* help move the probe in the right direction. The thrusters help to accurately point the probe's radio antenna to Earth, and to precisely point onboard experiments at objects, such as **stars**, to detect radio signals from them. *Cassini* will not return to Earth.

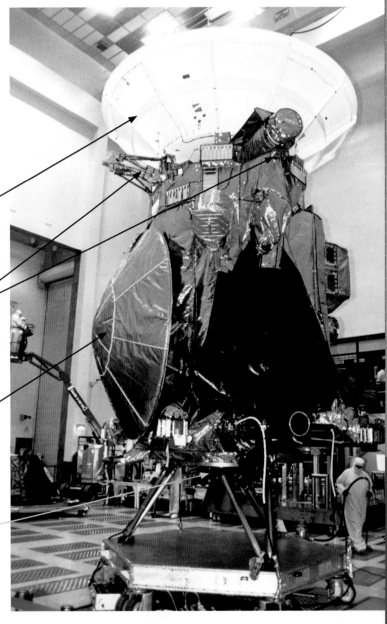

radio antenna
The antenna sends and receives communications from controllers on Earth and from the lander.

sensors
Sensors detect light, energy, **magnetic** fields, dust, gas, radio waves, and electrical charges. The probe also has cameras and radar to take images of and scan objects in space.

Huygens **lander**
Huygens was released from *Cassini* to land on Saturn's moon, Titan.

rocket thrusters

What's next?

In the future, space probes will be made from super light, thin materials which fold up for launching and unfurl when in space. The probes will be powered on their journey by huge solar panels.

Landers

A lander carries crew and equipment from an orbiting space probe to the surface of a moon or planet.

Where used?

Landers have visited the surfaces of Earth's moon and the planet Mars.

How used?

On reaching the surface of the planet or moon, landers transmit information on weather, atmosphere, and soil back to the orbiting probe and to Earth. Some landers return to their orbiting mother space probe carrying astronauts or soil samples.

Materials

Landers are made from materials such as **fiberglass**, graphite fiber, and the metal titanium. These materials are chosen for their light weight, strength and durability.

? Moon landers

On July 20 1969, the *Apollo II* lunar lander transported two astronauts from the orbiting rocket to the surface of the moon. Neil Armstrong and Buzz Aldrin became the first humans to walk on the moon. To return to their rocket, the lower part of the lunar lander acted as a pad to launch the upper part of the lander.

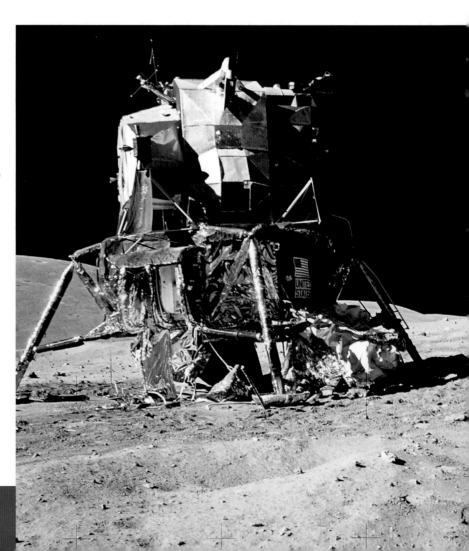

The lunar lander *Orion* during the *Apollo 16* mission to the Moon in 1972.

How do landers work?

When a lander is released by a space probe, the lander must withstand great heat. This heat is caused by the friction of the atmosphere rubbing against the lander as it enters the atmosphere at high speed. When the lander reaches the surface, motorized side petals enable it to move into an upright position. The petals open to form a ramp for an exploration vehicle called a rover to drive down. A lander and rover weigh 1,170 pounds (530 kg).

parachutes and air bags
Two parachutes and three air bags soften the landing.

heat shield
Underneath, the heat shield protects the lander from burning up as it enters the atmosphere.

side petals
Motors in the petals place the lander upright. The petals form a ramp for the rover.

inside the lander
The rover was stowed here. This photograph was taken after the rover had left the *Mars Spirit* lander to explore the surface of Mars.

What's next?

In the future, super-eye satellites will be placed in orbit around a planet. These satellites will relay images and information about the surface in a detail that can only currently be obtained by surface rovers.

Rovers

A rover is a vehicle that can be transported to the surface of a moon or planet to explore the terrain.

Where used?

In 1970, Russia placed an unmanned rover called *Lunokhod*, on Earth's moon. For months it sent information and television pictures to Earth. In 1971 and 1972, NASA astronauts drove a lunar roving vehicle (LRV) nicknamed a "moon buggy." In 2004, NASA placed two rovers, *Spirit* and *Opportunity*, on the surface of Mars. The rovers were designed to study the history of water on Mars.

How used?

Rovers transmit information, such as images of the landscape and chemicals detected, to the orbiting space probe and to Earth. Remote-controlled rovers make exploration safer for humans and enable information to be collected from planets that are too far for humans to currently travel to.

Materials

Rovers are made of metal alloys, such as platinum-rhodium, steel, and aluminum. They are insulated with a high-tech material, called aerogel. Other materials, such as glass and rubber, are also used. The materials are chosen because they are light and strong.

This view of the Mars landscape was transmitted from the rover *Opportunity* soon after it landed on January 24, 2004.

24

How do rovers work?

Rovers usually have wheels, video cameras, computers, sensors, mechanical arms to collect soil samples, and radio transmitters to send information back to the space probe orbiting the moon or planet. The probe relays this information to stations back on Earth. Rovers also have receivers so they can be controlled by radio signals sent from Earth.

cameras
Nine cameras on different parts of the rover give a wide-ranging view of the terrain.

antennas
Radio receivers enable the rover to be controlled by radio signals sent from Earth. Transmitters enable it to send data and images back to the orbiting space probe, which then relays images to Earth.

solar panels
Solar panels are used to generate electricity to power the rover.

instruments
Instruments help the rover to collect information. A robot arm collects soil samples. A spectrometer is used to measure the **electromagnetic** energy, such as light intensity and X rays. Other instruments detect the chemical composition of the planet, such as iron in the soil.

This is a computer illustration of the *Spirit* rover in its exploration of Mars.

What's next?

In the future, two-legged striders called bipods may walk on the surface of the planets or moons.

Satellites

Satellites are placed in Earth orbit to perform tasks, such as relaying television signals, or taking images of clouds to predict the weather on Earth.

Where used?

Satellites are launched by rocket or shuttle and placed in **geostationary orbit** 22,000 to 24,000 miles (35,000 to 38,000 km) high above Earth's equator. Satellites travel at the same speed as Earth rotates. This allows the satellite's antennae to be pointed straight at a satellite dish on Earth to send and receive signals.

Satellites are used for communications and observation.

How used?

Satellites are used mainly for communications, weather forecasting, finding resources, and for spying.

- Communications satellites relay telephone and television signals
- Weather forecast satellites are used to predict floods, storms, and hurricanes. They record **digital** images using visible light by day, and **infrared light** by night
- Resources satellites map temperature, pollution, crop disease, minerals, and water depth
- Spy satellites provide early warning of enemy activity. They can detect people, vehicles, and ships at sea

Materials

Satellites are made from strong, light metal alloys. Solar panels made from silicon make electricity to run the equipment on the satellite. Nitrogen is used to fuel the rocket thrusters.

How do satellites work?

Satellites have on-board computers, a power source, such as solar panels, small rocket boosters to help them point the right way and stay in orbit, and antennae to send and receive signals. Most satellites can be controlled from Earth.

The small amount of gravity in space near Earth (called micro-gravity) stops satellites from spinning into space.

radio transmitter and receiver
Radio and television waves travel in a straight line from their source, such as TV stations. Communications satellites reflect them back to Earth at an angle, broadcasting them around the world.

rocket thrusters

solar panels
The electricity generated by the solar panels is stored in batteries.

computer

What's next?

In the future, satellites will be able to see in high enough detail to distinguish people's faces. The military may use satellites that can detect and stop enemy missiles before they reach their target.

Space telescopes

Space telescopes combine a telescope with a satellite. Space telescopes can move and navigate in orbit, using rocket thrusters to change their course as they explore the universe.

Where used?

Space telescopes are placed in Earth orbit. The first space telescope was launched in the 1960s. In 1990, NASA and the European Space Agency used a shuttle to launch the Hubble Space Telescope. In 1993, Japan launched a telescope named Astro-D.

How used?

? Hubble Space Telescope facts

- Length: 43.3 feet (13.2 m)
- Width: 13.8 feet (4.2 m)
- Weight: 11 tons (11 tonnes)
- Orbit: 342–380 miles (550–612 km) above Earth
- Orbits Earth: every 97 minutes
- Orbital speed: 16,990 miles (27,359 km) per hour
- Lifespan: 20 years

Space telescopes record X rays and infrared and ultraviolet radiation from bodies in space. They then transmit this information to tracking stations on Earth. Placing a telescope in space enables signals to be detected more easily, because there is less interference from dust, wind, and water in Earth's atmosphere. Space telescopes have helped astronomers discover stars, galaxies, and other bodies in space.

Materials

The bodies of space telescopes are made mainly from metal alloys. The telescope has a glass lens with outside casings of heat-resistant plastic.

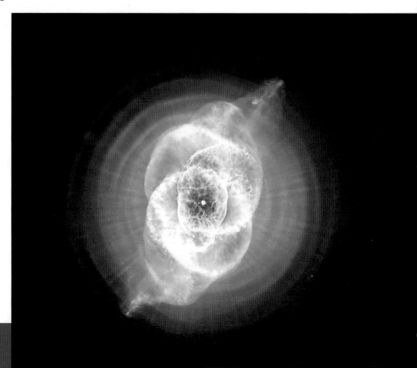

This body in space, called the Cat's-Eye Nebula, was seen by the Hubble Space Telescope in 2004.

How does the Hubble Space Telescope work?

Hubble travels in an elliptical orbit 342 to 380 miles (550 to 612 km) above Earth. This space telescope is 50 times more sensitive than ground-based telescopes, and its images have ten times the amount of information. Even though it travels at 16,990 miles (27,359 km) per hour, the telescope continually points at the same position in space. It does this by using an automatic guidance system that navigates by the stars.

door flap

antenna
The telescope has two antennas that send and receive signals from Earth.

telescope

guidance sensors
These help the telescope to navigate and point in the right direction.

solar panels

computer

cameras
The telescope has a lot of equipment for making images, such as a wide-field camera, a faint-object camera, infrared camera, and an imaging spectrograph.

What's next?

NASA is planning an 82-foot (25-m) lightweight telescope which can be folded, placed in a canister, launched, and inflated when it reaches space. This telescope may capture images that are 3,000 times sharper than the Hubble Space Telescope. In the future, telescopes may be built on the far side of Earth's moon. This would shield them from signals from Earth and would enable them to detect radio signals from other galaxies, stars and, perhaps, intelligent life.

How well does it work?

In this book you have read about and looked at the designs of many different technologies. As well as understanding how technology works, we also need to think about how well it works in relation to other needs, such as aesthetic, environmental, and social needs. We can judge how well the idea, product, or process works by considering questions, such as:

Manufacture	• Is the manufacture of the technology efficient in its use of energy and resources?
Usability	• Does the technology do the job it is designed to do? • Is it safe to use? • Is it easy to use?
Social impact	• Does it have any negative effects on people?
Environmental impact	• Does using the technology have any environmental effects? • Does it create noise, cause pollution, or create any waste products?
Aesthetics	• Does the design fit into its surroundings and look attractive?

Thinking about these sorts of questions can help people to invent improved ways of doing things.

One day, space technology may enable people to live and work on the moon.

Glossary

alloys mixtures of metals

aluminum a strong, light metal which resists rust and conducts electricity and heat well

artificial made by humans, not nature

atmosphere the layers of gases that surround a planet or moon

digital information stored in the form of numbers, called binary code

Earth orbit an orbit around Earth

electromagnetic a combination of waves of electric and magnetic fields carrying energy from one place to another—light, heat, microwaves, X rays, and radio waves are all different wavelengths of electromagnetic radiation

escape velocity 25,000 miles (40,000 km) per hour, the speed rockets must reach to escape the pull of Earth's gravity

fiberglass a strong, light material made by weaving and gluing strings of glass together

galaxy a large system of stars—the Solar System is in the Milky Way galaxy

geostationary orbit orbit where an object appears to stay in the same place above the Earth because it is traveling at the same speed as Earth rotates

gravity a force that pulls objects back to the surface of Earth

infrared light a wavelength of electromagnetic radiation that is invisible to the human eye

insulating reducing the amount of heat that gets through

laser a highly focused beam of light which can produce immense heat and power when focused at close range

magnetic able to attract iron or steel objects

moon a natural object that revolves around a planet

NASA (National Aeronautics and Space Administration) the US agency responsible for exploring space

orbiting revolving around an object in space

payload cargo

planet a body in space that orbits a star, and which does not shine its own light

Quaoar the 10th planet in the Solar System

radio receivers devices that detect radio signals

silicon a substance found in sand, clay, and many minerals, and used in computer chips, alloys, and building materials

solar panels large, flat panels that change sunlight into electricity

Solar System the sun and everything that orbits it, including Earth

stars huge, hot balls of gas in space—the sun is the closest star to Earth

Index